This book belongs to:

_____

_____

This book is designed to encourage small children to talk about what they see in the colourful pictures. Some simple questions have been suggested, but many more can be made up.

Always try to find a quiet space to share this book with your child. Children will be generous with their responses if you encourage them and give them confidence. They so quickly learn new words and love to use them. A good vocabulary helps them to think and enables them to express their thoughts.

Most importantly, enjoy the book together.

Written by Kath Jewitt
Illustrated by Claire Henley
Language consultant: Betty Root

This is a Parragon book
First published in 2005
Parragon, Queen Street House, 4 Queen Street
Bath, BA1 1HE, UK
Copyright © Parragon 2005

ISBN 1-40544-451-7
Printed in China

My First Book of...

TRACTORS

p

Tractors do lots of important jobs on the farm.

Find three tractors in the picture.

These tractors are off
to work for the day.

What colour is each tractor?

Tractors have big fat wheels.
The wheels help them to
drive over muddy,
bumpy ground.

How many wheels does this tractor have?

CHUG! CHUG! CHUG!

Tractors make a loud noise when they drive along.

The farmer is mending the tractor's engine.
Point to the tractor's engine.

Point to the tractor's steering wheel.

Every day the tractor needs to be filled with diesel to make it go.

This is the farmer's wife. What is she doing?

This tractor is pulling a plough.

The plough breaks up the soil ready for planting.

How many birds can you see in the picture?

The farmer is unloading sacks of seeds to plant in the field.

Look at the pictures on the sacks. What do you think the farmer is going to plant?

The farmer is taking vegetables
to market in the trailer.

What vegetables can you see in the trailer? What fruit can you see in the picture?

Tractors are very strong.
They can push and pull
heavy things.

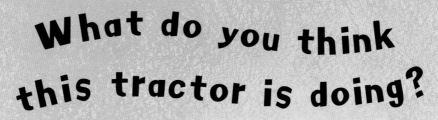

What do you think
this tractor is doing?

This tractor is driving through the snow with a load of hay.

Who do you think the hay is for?

Tractors get very muddy working in the fields.

What is the farmer doing?

At the end of the day,
the farmer puts the
tractor away in its shed.

Would you like to be a farmer
and drive a tractor?